D1601124

The Protestant Voice in American Pluralism

George H. Shriver
Lecture Series
in Religion
in American History
No. 2

THE PROTESTANT VOICE IN AMERICAN PLURALISM

Martin E. Marty

The University of Georgia Press
Athens & London

© 2004 by the University of Georgia Press
Athens, Georgia 30602
All rights reserved
Designed by Louise OFarrell
Set in 10/16 Aldus
Printed and bound by Thomson-Shore
The paper in this book meets the guidelines for
permanence and durability of the Committee on
Production Guidelines for Book Longevity of the
Council on Library Resources.

Printed in the United States of America

08   07   06   05   04   C   5   4   3   2   1

Library of Congress Cataloging-in-Publication Data
Marty, Martin E., 1928–
The Protestant voice in American pluralism / Martin E. Marty.
p. cm. — (George H. Shriver lecture series in religion
in American history ; no. 2)
Includes index.
ISBN 0-8203-2580-5 (alk. paper)
1. Protestantism—United States—History.
2. Religious pluralism—United States—History.
3. United States—Church history. I. Title. II. Series.
BR515.M327 2004
281'.4'0973—dc22
2003017196

British Library Cataloging-in-Publication Data available

CONTENTS

FOREWORD

The George H. Shriver Lectures: Religion in American History is an endowed series of lectures at Stetson University established by Dr. George Shriver, Professor of History Emeritus at Georgia Southern University. An alumnus of Stetson, Dr. Shriver created this lecture series to honor his alma mater and to enhance the understanding of religion's role in American society, both past and present. So that the lectures reach a wider audience, Dr. Shriver's endowment provides assistance for the publication of each lecture series. An author and professor for forty-one years, Dr. Shriver has received several awards during his career, both for his teaching and his scholarly publications. Among his numerous publications are his books *Philip Schaff: Christian Scholar and Ecumenical Prophet* and *Pilgrims through the Years: A Bicentennial History of First Baptist Church, Savannah, Georgia,* as well as *Contemporary Reflections on the Medieval Christian Tradition* and *Dictionary of Heresy Trials in American History,* which he edited, and *From Science to Theology,* which he translated.

The speaker for the 2002 Shriver Lectures, delivered on January 30–31, 2002, was Dr. Martin E. Marty, widely recognized as one of the most insightful analysts of the American religious landscape. Dr. Marty is the Fairfax M. Cone Distinguished Service Professor Emeritus at the University of Chicago, where he taught for thirty-five years. An ordained minister in the Evangelical Lutheran Church, Dr. Marty served for a decade as a parish pastor before joining the University of Chicago faculty, where he specialized in late-eighteenth- and twentieth-century American religion. A renowned historian, popular speaker, and frequent commentator on American religion, Dr. Marty is also a prolific author, having written over fifty books, including the three-volume *Modern American Religion*. Among his numerous awards and honors are the National Humanities Medal in 1997, the National Book Award in 1972 (for *Righteous Empire*), the Medal of the American Academy of Arts and Sciences in 1995, the University of Chicago Alumni Medal, and the Distinguished Service Medal of the Association of Theological Schools.

Under the title *The Protestant Voice in American Pluralism*, Dr. Marty's Shriver Lectures trace the changing face of religion in America from colonial times to the present. In his first lecture, Dr. Marty examines the characteristics of American Protestantism and the broader "Protestant culture" that dominated the country's history until approximately the last half century. His last two lectures provide an analysis of how that Protestant hegemony has been altered in the last fifty years, as the country has become more ethnically and religiously pluralistic. In his concluding remarks, Dr. Marty offers his audience and readers a brief suggestion for the role that Protestants, no longer the dominant force, can still play in the culture of which they are a part.

An enormous debt of gratitude is owed to Dr. Shriver for his generosity in endowing this lecture series. Through his own scholarly writings he has enriched our understanding of the past; through his endowment he has enriched the future of the university and those who hear and read these lectures. George and his wife Cathy made the presentation of these lectures by Dr. Marty even more meaningful by their presence, and for that we are grateful. Thanks are expressed also to the following: Dr. H. Douglas Lee, President of Stetson University, for his appreciation and support of the lecture series; Professor Kevin O'Keefe of the Department of History at Stetson, who serves on the Shriver Lectures Committee and helped plan and implement the lectures; Lisa Guenther and Colleen Becker for attending to the numerous details necessary to the lectures and the visit by Dr. Marty; and Nicole Mitchell and Sarah McKee of the University of Georgia Press.

> *Mitchell G. Reddish*
> *Chair, George H. Shriver Lectures Committee*
> *Stetson University*

PREFACE

The custodians of the George H. Shriver Lectures asked me to
address and juxtapose two themes that have been foci of my
studies in American religion and culture for decades: Protestantism and Pluralism.

This I have done in the lectures that here are transformed
into a book. In the nature of such cases, much of the original
oral style characterizes the work. We historians often write
stories with a technical background and cast, books "whose
footnotes have footnotes." When we are invited onto the public platform, those footnotes have to stay back home. To try
to convert three lectures into a technical genre violates both
the intentions of the original presentation and the nature of
the technical work. As I wrote these chapters, it often occurred
to me that one could carry generalizations from many para-
graphs into book-length elaborations. But the short book
based on lectures has its distinct function, and I hope this one
fulfills something of it: that is, to start or advance a conversation between town and gown, among academics and citizens
at large. These may not be the times wherein we have a sufficient sense of settled answers to argue on their basis. Argument is indeed grounded in answers that we advance by logic,

rhetoric, and devices. In argument there must be a winner, or someone who regards him- or herself as a winner. But there often will be a sense that much has been left out, namely, the potential that acts of imagination might spring from the questions conversationalists bring. I do not know where pluralist tendencies will take us. I do know that we will be better off projecting them against the background of history rather than simply lining up ideological forces and firing away.

George H. Shriver has been an honored member of our religious-history profession for decades, and he has influenced many of us as we have chosen our topics or fleshed them out. It was a singular act of commitment to the profession, of regard for his mentors, and of faith in the public's interest to subsidize these lectures. Invited to deliver them at a time when three or four books with urgent deadlines were on the desk before me, I still could not resist putting my energies to work to address these topics and to honor the Shrivers. Let me also thank the Department of Religious Studies and the Department of History at Stetson University, which, after my third visit as a lecturer, is getting to feel like a "home away from home." Professor Mitchell G. Reddish has been a generous host and is now a dedicated editor, and I appreciate his efforts.

WHEN PROTESTANTS RAN THE SHOW

When Homogeneity Ruled, 1607 to 1955

P ROTESTANTS OF VARIOUS SORTS "ran the show" in the colonies that became the United States of America and in the nation after its formation. What "running the show" means is something I define a bit later. First I begin with a note of sympathy for readers, one that expresses the hope that I can be forgiven for an offense that surely accompanies this chapter.

Rationale for the Approach That Follows

The sympathy is for anyone who has to run along at the brisk pace I have to set. From 1607 to 1955 is 348 years. (I once wrote an exactly 500-page book on exactly 500 years of American history, *Pilgrims in Their Own Land,* and found enough well-conditioned readers who evidently kept the pace.) Now I am to cover those years, well over one-third of a millennium, in just fifty pages.

My sympathy goes out because I have had experience with rapidly paced efforts to impart knowledge. I attended a pre-theological school during World War II. We were being hurried through on an accelerated program because there was a ministerial shortage and the military needed chaplains. During the acceleration we were in a single course on the whole Hebrew Scriptures, the Old Testament. The professor spent a good deal of time on Genesis and Exodus, and book by book, he had to hasten the pace. Toward the end we got only snapshots of prophets. A classmate dropped a pencil, and he claimed that while he picked it up, he missed Nahum, Habakkuk, and Zephaniah.

Forgiveness? I need that from readers and fellow historians who are more used to close-ups, slices of history pictured from vantages where we can check up on each other. The span and scope of this chapter commit me to painting with such a broad brush that most detail gets left behind. Still, such an endeavor is not completely disadvantageous. A reconnaissance plane flying over a territory can discern things that do not fall into perspective by people on the ground. A satellite thirty thousand miles up can be of use to weather bureaus as they track the movement of a hurricane. What its cameras show as a result is not the only kind of scene and does not provide the only kind of knowledge that people in the path of the hurricane need. But that distinctive distant vision has its place.

The effort social historians make to cover a subject in great detail and up close can in fact work against attempts to present fuller pictures. Historian Page Smith once told some of us about a historian at the University of Wisconsin in Madison who received a full-length dissertation on a subject like "Dairy Farming in Southwest Monroe County, 1875–1878." He fired it back to the student with a simple comment: "You covered the subject teat by teat." He was ready to follow up, however, with critical comments of other sorts and with questions that demanded answering. Who owned the cows? The answer was Swiss Americans. Why did they come to America, to Wisconsin, to Monroe County? Where did their move fit into Euro-pean-American history? What were they thinking and saying as they embarked on their ventures in a new land?

A three-lecture-long or book-length study of the Protes-tant involvement against New York governor Al Smith in his 1928 presidential campaign could be of immense use. In its story we could get some grasp of anti-Catholicism, for Smith was a Catholic, or of Protestant political action, because so of-ten Protestants said they were not in politics. But if we have *only* such studies, we will not learn backgrounds, contexts, and consequences. So I ask for forgiveness from those who find the generalizations too huge and hope that the perspec-tive provided here will relate positively to more minute in-quiries by other historians, or by me, on other assignments.

Chronological Framing of the Theme

I begin with 1607 because that is the date of the first perma-nent settlement in what became the thirteen colonies. The

Virginia settlers at Jamestown were by no means the first Protestants to set foot on these shores, but they are the first who stayed. They were members of the Church of England, what today is called a part of the Anglican Communion. Some of their heirs in the Episcopal Church do not like to be listed as Protestant. They are members of the one, holy, *catholic*, and apostolic church. Their spiritual ancestors saw themselves as rightful descendants in the apostolic lineage, as reformers of one version of that church catholic, the Roman Catholic, that had gone astray.

We always have to take seriously the theological claims of anybody, so the Anglicans may be catholic, or merely Anglican. But to social scientists and most historians, looking on from a slight distance and not being called to make theological judgments, they were and are and will remain sociologically and, let me say, politically Protestant. So they are the pioneers, anteceding the Pilgrims and Puritans of Plymouth Colony and Massachusetts Bay in 1620 and 1630. And when the Reverend Robert Hunt presided at Communion along the James River in 1607, he was inaugurating non–Roman Catholic, indeed, Protestant worship and permanent presence here. (Protestants were not to have the southern colonies to themselves. In 1634 the founders of Maryland, though Catholic, arrived with a proprietary charter that was open to the presence of other faiths. However, Protestants soon caught on to what was happening, and Maryland also became Anglican, Protestant.)

As for the terminal date of 1955, I have chosen something symbolic, and the choice may seem arbitrary, almost trivial. Though the period begins with intrepid adventurers on the high seas and the swampy bottoms along a Virginia river, it ends with, of all things, the publication of a book. That book is *Protestant-Catholic-Jew* by Jewish sociologist-theologian Will Herberg. I have reserved discussion of what Herberg's work symbolized as the turning-toward of pluralism for later. For the moment the book serves as an indicator of the way Protestantism now had to share place, not only thanks to statistical shifts but also in the ethos and power relations in American life.

Can a book serve this way? Symbolically, yes. Books like Herberg's do not start wars, initiate peace pacts, or inaugurate new economic proposals. They do not have influence the same way the works of John Maynard Keynes or John Kenneth Galbraith or Milton Friedman had impact in the economic order. They do not make history the way Hitler's *Mein Kampf* or Marx's *Das Kapital* did. Yet their authors pick up diffuse strands of historical tendency, weave them into a whole, and cast the consequent fabric into the public arena where at least some grasp it and begin to redefine the world.

One could cite as roughly contemporary examples Rachel Carson's *Silent Spring* for its role in the environmental movement after 1962 or Betty Friedan's *The Feminine Mystique* and the coalescence of women's liberation forces after 1963. After Will Herberg wrote, more and more chroniclers and analysts began to speak of a post-Protestant age and the arrival of a pluralist challenge, if not replacement.

Definitions

The word "American" in the title unfairly rules out Canada and Central and South America and in this book refers simply to the United States and the thirteen colonies before its formation.

The word "religion," which I use throughout the book, dare not detain us long here. Often, to save space and time and get to the subject, I brush past the endless and usually legitimate debates about what "religion" means. I can provide book-length bibliographies that deal with arguments over that second-order word. By "second-order" I mean that most people speak instead of being born again or having found God or enlightenment or the Spirit, reserving the word "religion" for when a pollster asks, "What are you?"

We historians and social scientists, who may not be good at setting forth a priori definitions, tend to work the way phenomenologists do. That is, they come across phenomena, listen for what the phenomena get called, and draw some tentative conclusions about the makeup of those phenomena. Thus no historian to my knowledge woke up in the summer of 1920 and said, "Let's invent Fundamentalism and then go looking for what matches the meanings that term can acquire." Instead observers came across the rationale of a Baptist editor who worked during denominational battles that year.

He said, "Conservatives may be right, but they do not bestir themselves to come to the Lord's side for battle. Those of us who do, need a new name for our movement. We deal with fundamentals, so let us call ourselves Fundamentalists." As similar movements appeared elsewhere, the observers found patterns, syndromes, tendencies, and expressions that matched those related to the Baptist argument. So for all its faults, "Fundamentalism" it was.

So it is with "religion." The word appears only a few times in the King James Bible and once or twice in most Protestant hymnals. Yet to statisticians and pollsters, everyone must have *a* religion. So we pay attention to what they point to at such times. This is not the place to go into detail, but I have found six features to be virtual constants.

First, people have what Paul Tillich called "ultimate concern," the whole ball of wax, the whole ball game, that by which they live and for which they die. Not all ultimate concern has to be seen religiously, but everything called religion finds people preoccupied with some version of ultimate concern.

To that add two features. We tend to call discourse religious if those who engage in it prefer mythic and symbolic language to straight-out practical and ordinary prose. And we find actions religious if the same people also ritualize and render ceremonial many themes that need marking: birth, marriage, and death; the seasons in the life of nature and the gods; the events in the life of God revealed among people.

Next comes what I call a quasi-metaphysical backdrop. This term refers to the way people we call religious sense, experience, testify to, or act on the basis of the notion or claim that behind the events and thoughts and doings in the ordinary world there is an extraordinary backdrop. Such people do not tolerate the merely random and chaotic but tend to find patterns of meaning, usually pointing to a transcendent order. Forces or Persons act upon them, and they must respond.

After this come behavioral correlates. If you believe this, then you will not drink that, but you will eat this; you will deal thus with your possessions and may have to try to convert others.

Finally—and this is being tested in the late-modern world—those who relate to these five tend to seek and find some form of communal expression. They form or join congregations, denominations, movements, cells, action groups. Modern individualized spirituality is challenging this dimension, but overall, communalism has the privileged position around the globe.

Now for my brisk, flip way of clearing the ground and getting to the point: I was one of eight editors of the sixteen-volume *Encyclopedia of Religion*. At every meeting and in correspondence we all had to make the case for why a certain term belonged, while another did not. I define religion as the kind of stuff you write about in a book with that title. American Protestants form a subset of "religion, people" in American history.

Another phrase, used in this chapter's title, is "run the show." In one of my dictionaries, definition number 28 relates "run" to "manage, control, direct." Of course, Protestants did not "run the show" the way the U.S. Supreme Court and lesser courts "manage" the laws. They did not "control" the way the police can and usually do. They may have done some directing, but it was all by persuasion. Thus they ran the show the way barkers lure people to carnival shows or the way producers of the shows direct the onstage folk who need directors if they are to know what to do.

Does anyone after 1955 or so "manage, control, direct" American religion? Does the pope? Billy Graham? Any heads of councils of churches or associations of Evangelicals? Not likely. Certainly not through legal establishment or with legally sanctioned instruments of privilege. At one time, however, Protestants did have a larger role in running the religious show and, with it, many aspects of the legal show.

That leaves "show," as in "running the show." The connotation here is the carnival or circus and what goes on under the big tent we have chosen to call religion. Sociologist Peter Berger has spoken of *The Sacred Canopy* as arching over and protecting the phenomena of religion. Under it the many varieties of the religious coexist. To attract attention in a free society, its performing agents must "put on a show."

Such show-ing is not alien to religious traditions. In biblical speech God directs the people of God to show forth, demonstrate, illustrate, and exemplify the divine impetus among humans. Catholics reserve the Host, the consecrated bread that is the Body of Christ, in a "monstrance," a holder that shows "what's going on, what's to be observed." A performance is a show. Religions contribute to the Big Show that is America, and among them, Protestantism once managed, controlled, and directed what went on among the vast majority of the people, at least the religious people. No more.

Three Locations of Protestants and Protestantisms

When I speak of Protestants, I refer to at least four phenomena or expressions. First, in America, the term naturally includes all the denominations that make up the genus "Protestant." One might think of these denominations in four clusters. First are the "colonial big three": the Anglicans of the southern colonies, who later came to be called Episcopalian; the northern colonial heirs of Puritanism, the New England Congregationalists who today are part of the ancestry of the United Church of Christ; and the mainly midcolony later arrivals who prospered without establishment, the Presbyterians in their many forms and branches.

The second cluster includes those groups who, in my line of thinking, though originally dissenters, would later succeed on the frontier, as citizens moved west. First among these are the Baptists, northern and southern, most of whom issued from the Rhode Island founders and post-Congregationalists who moved west across the mountains and south, to dominate a region as few other versions of Protestantism did in the Southern Baptist Convention. With them came the Methodists, weakened and under suspicion soon after their arrival as dissenters from the Anglicans, and the homegrown Christians of the Disciples of Christ and some corollary denominations, all of whom prospered on the frontier.

The third set of peoples whom no one questions in respect to their Protestant credentials consists of the heirs of the continental European migrants who spoke other than English. They arrived first in the middle colonies of Pennsylvania, New Jersey, and New York and then came directly to the Midwest and other regions. These included the German and Dutch Reformed of New York and later of Michigan, Iowa, and the like, and the Lutherans from Scandinavia and Germany, who settled in the middle colonies but then came to be a strong presence especially in the Upper Midwest. Also included in this group are the Anabaptists, the Mennonites, the Amish, the Church of the Brethren, and others like them.

Finally, the fourth cluster, who had a smaller role in running the show, consists of the Pentecostal and other charismatic groups that rose in the beginning of the twentieth century and burgeoned in its second half. By 1955 they were not well enough positioned in social class and ethos to be dominant, but they learned the rules of the game belatedly and acquired much power in the period when pluralism characterized the American scene.

I have not included the huge cluster of Methodists, Baptists, and Pentecostals, multimillion-membered strong and unquestionably Protestant, who are African Americans, because through 1955 they had no chance to help run the show. They were very effective in managing, controlling, and directing blacks religiously, but they had little power or influence beyond them in the centuries of slavery and segregation that preceded the civil rights movement, which came at the end of the Protestant dominance.

Second, having cited some of the members of the denominational grouping, I speak of "Protestantism" in connection with all the people who designate themselves as such or who are designated as such by pollsters and social scientists. These are the individuals who are not Catholic or Orthodox or Jewish or Mormon or Muslim but who get typed as Protestant unless they insist that they have no religion or no preference. They are not ordinarily mobilizable in any ecclesiastical or political way but in some senses make up a large unorganized cohort under the Protestant canopy and play their own anomalous role in the Protestant "show."

Third, alongside the denominational and unaffiliated Protestant people is Protestant culture. This is a kind of penumbra, aura, ethos, or effect that appears in the speech, action, and thought of Americans who do not mind being called Protestant as opposed to anything else or who get called that because they have an "ethic" others call Protestant or because they are "anti-" something else, such as Catholic.

Before the symbolic date of 1955 these three types of

peoples ran the show, managing, controlling, or directing, however wanly or subtly, however boldly and frontally, in diverse ways.

Think first of the dominance Protestants have in the roll call of all denominations in America. Roman Catholicism has its main branch, loyal to the pope, and a couple of spin-offs, "Polish Catholic" and the like. Orthodoxy sees itself as one, divided by geography and jurisdiction into autocephalic churches like the Romanian, the Russian, and the Greek. Jews come in four or five denominational forms. The rest of the yearbooks and phone books belong to over two hundred easily recognized denominations and listings called Protestant. Those denominations were best poised to run something.

Second are the individual Protestants. Some of them are Protestant only in that they lean toward Protestantism and own a map to guide them to a Protestant church for their daughters' wedding site. Others find participation in Protestantism, whether they call their affiliation by that name or not, the be-all and end-all of their religious participation. They park their ultimate concern and all that connects with it there.

The third, Protestant culture, is more complex, elusive, hard to define or point to. In economics, this culture is the "Protestant ethic." In politics, it has to do with the Protestant character of the American Enlightenment among "founders" who shaped the legal fabric. Among poets and writers, artists and musicians, it is part of a theme devoted to the Bible, to "grace," to "works of love and justice."

In 1927 a French visitor, André Siegfried, would note and speak of the United States as a Protestant country and culture (see his book *America Comes of Age*). No other designation served as well. In the years that followed, theologian H. Richard Niebuhr, as he wrote of *The Kingdom of God in America*, would cite Siegfried and agree with him.

So the nation was Protestant. So Protestants managed, controlled, and directed much of American religious culture and society in general. But there are ironies:

Unlike most managing, controlling, and directing agencies, Protestantism is hard to define, not easy to locate, and almost impossible to relate to in a coherent way.

At the same time, though it is statistically dominant to this day, Protestantism lacks a constituency. It does not summon loyalties, though it once might have. People might call themselves Protestant or let others call them that, but they think of themselves as religious or Christian or Bible believing or United Methodist before they think of themselves as Protestant. They pay no dues and give few alms to anything called Protestant. It is hard to find Protestant entities in most phone books. They attract few loyalties.

As someone sometimes summoned by publishers, conference planners, and mass communicators to write about or speak on behalf of Protestantism, I would have to say that it lacks constituencies. Some years ago a publisher was producing a multivolume work on religions: Manichaeism, Scandinavian religion, the "high" religions, and the like. I was assigned *Protestantism* and dutifully wrote a generally well-reviewed book with that breathtakingly exciting title. It sold the requisite number of copies, passed into paperback before it passed on to the Great Beyond called "Returns" or "Out of Print," and disappeared, except from libraries. What I noticed was that it was seen as a reference book more than a chronicle of a living movement. A book on Mormons or Quakers would be controversial no matter what it said. But one must *do* something to sell the Protestant concept.

One way to do that is to put the word into a subtitle. In 1970 I published *Righteous Empire* and, after the colon, tucked away *The Protestant Experience in America.* What caught the imagination and stirred controversy was the dual set of concepts "righteous" and "empire," for it was a story of managing, controlling, and directing by the people today called mainline Protestants. (It did not deal much with the neo-Evangelicals of the twentieth century who became Evangelicals for one reason: The publisher had assigned the history of Evangelicals to another historian who never finished his portion of this bicentennial series. Ever after, I have not been able to speak as if mainline equals Protestant, but must always include groups once seen as challengers, dissenters, folks "at the margin," like Seventh-Day Adventists, and the once overlooked, like African American Protestants.)

Features of the Protestant Skeleton

In the book *Protestantism* and in encyclopedia articles, I have on occasion been called on to define Protestantism. Some elements in its skeleton include the following:

First, it is the main form of Western Christianity that is not under the Roman obedience. "Obedience" is a harsh-sounding term, and people who use it do not intend to be pejorative—at least this user does not want to stigmatize by suggesting obeisance and fealty. Still, to be a Catholic is to be connected through faith and authority to the Catholic hierarchical system and the bishop of Rome, the pope. Not to recognize papal authority is to rule one's self out of the Roman (Western) Catholic church. Protestants may be friendly to Catholicism and popes, but by definition they are not of that obedience.

Next, obviously, being Western, they are not Eastern Christians; they are not Orthodox.

Continuing from there to list many elements that all Protestants claim or do or do not do that no one else claims or does or does not do would be nice, but it's difficult. Two features from the sixteenth-century conflicts stand out as candidates, and before, say, 1955, they both went further than they do now.

The first of these is scriptural authority. The Protestants often say they adhere to the theme of *sola scriptura*, the Bible alone. It is the source and norm of their beliefs, the text from which their teachings and their controversies both grow. Several things have happened, however.

For one thing, though Catholics are not devoted to *sola*, because they recognize the formal magisterial authority of church tradition, they are more *scriptural* than they were in the years of Protestant hegemony. The Second Vatican Council (1962–65) demonstrated how much devotion to biblical scholarship, reading, and authority was developing in Catholicism.

Add to this the fact that the rise of biblical criticism in the nineteenth century has led many Protestants to be less sure of the sole and clear authority of the Bible. Couple this with the development of hermeneutics in the twentieth century, and one finds Protestants of many sorts wavering in their claim that *sola scriptura* settles everything. The hermeneuticians noted that every interpreter and every interpreting community brings preunderstandings and often implicit precommitments to the reading of any text, including the biblical. Hermeneutics then introduced the concept of subjectivity and, some thought, relativism, or at least perspectivism, to biblical criticism.

Many Fundamentalists, Evangelicals, and conservative Baptists challenge the hermeneuticians when they insist that they come naked and without presuppositions to the Bible and let it simply speak to them, because it is clear and perspicuous. To others, however, such an argument seems faulty. Fundamentalists who bring Anabaptist adult- or believer-baptism commitments to biblical texts on baptismal subjects face Fundamentalists who bring (e.g., Presbyterian) regenerative- and infant-baptism views. They both study the same texts, molecule of ink by molecule of ink, yet they come out near where they started, do not switch camps, do not say to the other "you were right all along!" or "we cry uncle!" or "thanks for correcting us." Outside observers say that hermeneutical principles are at stake and we must look beyond simply *sola scriptura* to see what goes into the Protestant makeup and set of decisions.

Alongside that scriptural principle—which remains *very* strong, even though it cannot mean quite the same thing it did a century ago—Protestants give lip service and often well-intentioned and variously informed commitments to the material principle that stresses divine grace as the agency of human faith and response. This they assert against the notion that the believer somehow cooperates in salvation or partly achieves it through merits or works. Surely, that ought to remain as a mark that only Protestants and all Protestants believe!

Not so quick, say questioners within and beyond Protestantism. First, historians are now apt to say that many elements in Catholicism stressed grace, unmerited mercy, and the divine gift before the Protestants came along. Catholicism may have cluttered divine grace with other misfit teachings (e.g., the selling of indulgences and Pelagian-type proclamations about human capability and cooperation), but it was there. Post-Reformation Tridentine (after the Council of Trent) Catholicism may have reacted with hard lines that further obscured this ancient and durable teaching, but it won its way back.

By the time of the Second Vatican Council more and more Protestants recognized the renewal and triumph of grace in

Roman Catholicism. By October 1998 most Lutherans of the world signed on to an official declaration with the Vatican on justification by faith, the controverted teaching in the sixteenth century. This represented the burying of the ax heads, if not the handles. Many on both sides found reason to hang on to the handles to do a bit of nudging, nightstick swinging, and maybe sneaky bludgeoning—which is a way of saying that by no means did the two sides agree on all accents and nuances—but it is very hard for Protestants to claim successfully that they alone are the grace-and-faith-not-works people in Western Christianity.

For that matter, the televangelist listener or sermon reader, to say nothing of one who observes market-oriented, busy Protestants, will find the message of grace compromised in many of the messages and practices. The injunction to tithe, which means, "Send in money to the televangelist," usually comes connected with a merits, works, or earning theme. Many sermonic injunctions end with moralistic and legalistic "you gottas"—you have to do this or that. Where, critics ask, has grace gone in such expressions?

Maybe it is time to draw a tentative conclusion about some consequences of these exceptions, waverings, mutual influences, and syncretisms. Here is a sample, radical sounding though it be:

In 2002 Protestantism does not exist. The word always needs adjectives, three sets of which have emerged as part of the conventional wisdom by members, mass communicators, strategists, social scientists, theologians, and pop culturalists alike. There are instead:

1. mainline, mainstream, or standard-brand Protestants, with whom about 25 percent of the American people line up;

2. Evangelical Protestants, including Pentecostals, Fundamentalists, and conservative-type Baptists, in a cohort of 25 percent of the American "preferrers," who make up a more energetic and kinetic element today; and

3. African American Protestants, consisting of the 8 percent of American people who identify with black Protestantism.

Even to speak of these three factions is to gloss over enormous differences within the camps. (And, let us not forget, there are many crossovers. The Protestant left of the right and right of the left, which is not the center, is a force with which to reckon. That is, Evangelicals of open sensibility often link with mainliners who find common sources with them in their own longer traditions, and both connect with blacks, to form a kind of viscous front.)

Historian George Marsden, for example, wrote a history of a flagship Evangelical theological school, Fuller Seminary in California. It is as fine a history of a seminary as I have read. What surprised many readers was its story of profound controversy among founders and followers over basic theological themes. What had looked like a phalanx, a solid front, a wedge driven into the mainline ranks, was a history of conflict, fissures, and tensions. Moreover, I recall a review by a New York Hispanic Pentecostal intellectual, who also liked the book. But he said, in effect, "Every name in the index of this book (with the exception of those who had been rejected as un-Evangelical by Fullerites) refers to someone I'd call Evangelical or to someone who would call me Evangelical. Those with whom I worship and work would call everyone in the index Evangelical. And yet, we have *vast* differences." The Pentecostals and Hispanics in general did not share and could not come to share the Reformed scholastic metaphysical position on which Fuller had been erected.

What was interesting was that neither group used the word "Protestant" to describe themselves, though both are focally Protestant. All mainline Protestants would have called all the people indexed in Marsden's book Protestant, and all the people in Marsden's book would call mainliners Protestant (though they may not and would not always call all of them Christian!). Yet there were even more vast differences between these groups.

Given the diffusion of definitional features and the factions that divide Protestantism—most of them anticipated a half century before 1955—how should we perceive that in any way Protestants ran the show, managing, controlling, and directing anything?

Protestant *Creencias:*
The Beliefs That We *Are*

Eight themes can provide some clues. Each of them falls into the category of what Spanish philosopher José Ortega y Gasset called *creencias.* Traces of that Spanish word exist in our own words "creed" and "credo," a tip-off that belief is involved. For Ortega, however, *creencias* are not so much ideas that people *have* but the ideas that people *are;* not the beliefs people *hold* but those by which they are *held.* Every culture tends to have several hard-to-define *creencias.* They need not be a large number and probably cannot be. We may *hold* all kinds of beliefs, but we cannot *be* so many.

Thus Presbyterians, as Calvinists, believe in double predestination, the doctrine that affirms that God predestines some individuals to salvation and, hence, others to condemnation. Yet whoever deals with the bowling team of the Presbyterian Church on the corner or with a social action front of the Presbyterian Church in the United States or discusses philosophies of life with a friendly neighborhood Presbyterian would be hard pressed to find even archeological remains of this teaching in the *actual* Presbyterian faith and life. Most Presbyterians will give lip service to such a teaching when reminded of it. Many of them may genuinely profess their faith when pressed on controversial catechismal or denominational terms, but so many other compromising teachings have since entered the Presbyterian communion in practical living that a formal doctrine of divine foreknowledge or double predestining no longer plays a significant role in the *creencias*. The same is true of many other faiths. The author of a doctoral study of the annual volume of sample sermons sent out by the publishing house of a superorthodox Lutheran group went looking for what that church body would consider "pure" preaching of the justification-by-faith theme that is supposed to be constitutive of Lutheranism. It appeared in only two or three of the exemplary sermons. Again, every preacher believed in that creedal teaching, but it was shrouded by overgrowths of complementary, supplementary, and sometimes conflicting beliefs that went into the communicants' *creencias*. Such examples are not meant to track evidences of bad faith or hypocrisy, however, but rather are meant to demonstrate that though certain distinguishing beliefs may exist historically, they are not necessarily the elements that amount to a Protestant deposit in the culture.

First among the eight *creencias* that I would suggest do apply is that God is the Lord of history, the sovereign of nations, the hidden and sometimes manifest agent of this nation's history. American Protestantism is very much *American* Protestant. That is as true of the Protestants who as a group could not run the show—African Americans or dirt-poor backcountry southern Baptists—as it is of the white elites and stocks-rich downtown or suburban southern Baptists who still wield considerable power.

Though the New England Puritans are best known and

most credited for infusing (or blighting) the nation with the notion that it is "under God," almost everyone else pitched in. Today it would be hard to sort most Catholics and most Jews out of the "under God" confessors. Perhaps this would have still been the profession had Catholics been the main shapers of American religion from 1607 to almost the present, yet their concept of how this sovereignty is mediated through the church, through *The* Church, would have differed vastly from the individualized perception, reception, and response of Protestants from the 1620s to the 1950s and later.

The concept held by many in the Protestant-believing communities that they were somehow God's New Israel, God's new people, is an American notion, one that helps define the nation. A half century ago one of my thesis advisers was Daniel J. Boorstin, later Librarian of Congress. Though he was a conservative legal scholar, he chafed that there was a House Un-American Activities Committee, then in its prime. He asked us, "Can you picture a House Un-Canadian Activities Committee? A House Un-Luxembourgian Committee?"

That "un-" was a sign of a quite secularized complex from which the language of "under God" can be dredged. It is interesting that those two words were inserted into the Pledge of Allegiance in 1954, at the end of the era of Protestant hegemony, as Americans were trying to stay united in the midst of their newly realized pluralism. Would they have had that concept available were it not for the Protestant witness of individual and then communal response to the sovereign Lord of history, acting mysteriously?

Curiously but of great importance, Abraham Lincoln, that most Protestant of presidents and the only one of them who never joined a Protestant or any other church, dealt with this theme of the mysterious action of a God who holds humans responsible by invoking God in the most profound and sophisticated ways. He was a kind of Protestant who rose in the civil order to teach Protestant Americans how to be Protestant, even as both sides were forgetting what Protestant meant in the War between the States, even as both sides claimed God for their cause.

Much more complicated is the second of these *creencias*: the extension of this Lordship over history and the nation through Jesus Christ. Here, of course, the Protestant witness is separated from Jewish understandings, because Jesus can play no positive role in Jewish relations to environment and events. Here, of course, one notes that Jesus is present in Roman Catholicism but in somewhat different ways. For one thing, the Trinitarian accent is stronger in Catholicism than in most Protestantism. For another, Catholics have surrounded their covenanting with God with other agents. Most obviously, in major wars, leading Catholic hierarchs have commended America to Mary, Mother of God, Queen of Angels, benefactress of this nation. Jesus has been there but has had much company.

H. Richard Niebuhr, when he wrote of *The Kingdom of God in America,* noted this Christocentric feature. He went so far as to observe that those who were theologically Trinitarian Protestants often in practice were devoted to Jesus as if in a Unitarianism of the Second Person of the Trinity. (*Unitarian* Unitarianism concentrated on what Trinitarians called the First Person of the Trinity, the Creator, the divine Father.) The covenant of grace, which Calvinists, who promoted divine sovereignty, saw operative in the civil realm, was mediated through Christ. Lutherans, let it be noted in passing, were not major proponents of this *creencia,* because they related Jesus Christ more to the promise of salvation than to the running of the show in the civil and practical order. No one asked them, however, and in their rhetoric, many of them started sounding like Calvinists.

Much has happened to this *creencia* since the mid-1950s, so much that the near-unanimity with which Protestants held it when H. Richard Niebuhr was writing in 1936 is hard to picture. When Catholicism waned as the defining target against which mainline Protestants rallied—Pope John XXIII after 1958 removed that target once and for all, and quickly— such Protestants took recourse to their distinctive tradition less frequently while they worked on civil and political strategies. As pluralism came to be defined, they became more open to the presence of Jews on the domestic scene and have sometimes muffled their witness to Jesus as operating in the nation, whether in public prayer or conversation. The Christocentric element has been left to Evangelicals, particularly to those of late-Calvinist stamp, who set out to reclaim America for Christ, who seek through law and persuasion to want Jesus acknowledged with the crèche on the public's courthouse lawn in the civic square. They are the ones who want politicians to ask, "What would Jesus do?" Such witnesses are strong in American religion and politics today, and they trade on an aspect of the theological *creencias* deposited and formed by "all" Protestants, though they never speak for Protestantism as such any more.

The third *creencia* is freedom, individual freedom, the resort to conscience. Martin Luther was not seeking civil rights when he stood up to the pope and emperor in the name of biblically informed and reasonably persuaded individual conscience with his famed "Here I stand." So he is not so easily invoked civilly, however heroic his image often appears to be. But Martin Luther King Jr. stood in a long Protestant tradition, informed by even some recent exemplars—Walter Rauschenbusch, Reinhold Niebuhr, and the devotee of the "Protestant Principle," Paul Tillich—when he invoked conscience in the name of "higher law" for civil rights.

Significantly, however, though King could draw on the Protestant deposit, he now chose to, had to, diffuse it on interfaith and nonfaith grounds in pluralist America. His demonstrators included not only African American Protestants at the center but also Roman Catholics (even before rapprochements with the Protestants, thanks to Vatican II), Jews, and nonbelievers, openly acknowledged for their pursuit of free-dom on almost every ground *except* Christological.

The emphasis on freedom can be traced back to dissenters like the Baptists and Quakers in colonial New England and their descendants ever since. Catholics, however, though patri-ots, though good citizens, though giving few or no reasons for non-Catholics to be suspicious, for many creedal and eccle-siastical reasons, were not perceived by Protestants until the recent past to be prime *agents* in providing Jesus-centered, Christological bases for freedom.

A fourth element in the Protestant deposit among the *creencias* has to do with its influence in shaping what is hard to describe but what might here be designated the "voluntary church." Jews might be the "elect people," but when they ac-knowledge God and community, they have historically made little of choice. A half century ago a shocking book title was *Why I Choose to Be a Jew.* If you have a Jewish mother, you *are* a Jew, whether you observe or not. If you marry a non-Jew, the rabbis say, you are betraying the heritage of peoplehood.

Catholics today—I have heard them worrying about this at a conference as recently as 2001—are losing the "ontology of the church" in their daily outlook. So say historians and theo-logians who remember or point out that decades ago the church was prior to one's spirituality or preference or choice. It was just *there,* as a living divine presence. If your parents were Catholic, you were baptized and nurtured in the faith.

You might not always frequent mass or follow the book or be moved by canon law, but you belonged to the Catholic people and had to be somewhat strenuous about intentionally parting from them (as opposed to drifting in indifference).

For Protestants, as much as they depended on genes (godliness, says historian Edmund Morgan, was believed to pass through the loins of godly parents to godly children) or territory (e.g., Norwegian Lutheran, Scottish Presbyterian, southern Baptist) to predispose children to a faith tradition and community, the modern folk among them (ca. 1730) began to see that if a believing community was to exist tomorrow, the seniors had to convert their own children. Neighbors had to convert neighbors. Mainliners devoted themselves to this 250-year-old American understanding and languished. Evangelicals took to it with zest.

So the "Go to the Church of Your Choice" theme patented by billboard makers of Religion in American Life (RIAL) in the 1950s came to be part of the informal canon of *creencias*. Here Evangelicals are more modern, American, and decision and market driven than most other Protestants. "Are you born again?" "Have you made a decision for Christ?" "Have you found your *personal* Savior?" "What would Jesus do?" "If you were to die tonight, would you wake up in heaven?" Such questions have influence beyond the Evangelical Protestant camp. *People* magazine sometimes features "spiritual" and New Age movie stars who, having experienced a warm tingle in the bath or having been stunned by a guru at a weekend retreat, describe themselves as born again. But the born again tradition, the one that leads the evangelized, awakened, enlightened convert to "the church of her choice," or the home within the movement, is born of the earlier Protestant recognition that church life is voluntary, organized around persons who have made decisions and accepted a particular ideology. The difference between the now and the then is that the born again choice of voluntary participation (whether to participate, where to join) is diffused throughout the market-based competitive culture and is not a Protestant project as such.

Fifth, thanks to Protestant witness and example, *sola scriptura*, the biblical scripture, has its own place in the *creencias* of Americans. The Bible was the prototype that led Pilgrims to call themselves Pilgrims, that gave them and people far from their tradition the notion that America is God's New Israel, Zion, a city set upon a hill, a vineyard in which citizens are stewards. Today such themes are invoked on occasion patriotically and sometimes in disturbing ways to allies who are less sure that America is "scriptured" and "scripted."

The role of the Bible has been enormous. My teacher and colleague Jerald C. Brauer, writing at mid–twentieth century on *Protestantism in America*, insisted that Protestantism had two main marks. One, it was "scriptured," devoted to the Bible. Two, it was constantly ready to experiment. Brauer liked to quote pastor John Robinson, who bade farewell to the *Mayflower* Company as it headed west across the Atlantic with the affirmation that "the Lord hath more truth and light yet to break forth from his holy word."

Scripturalism spread. Start a movement, especially a religious one in America, and you had better have a text that scripts it. Numbers of scholars have traced the way far-from-Protestant movements in the sixties each owned and offered their text: *The Whole Earth Catalog, Divine Principle, The Autobiography of Malcolm X*, and many more. Not that these all were directly influenced by the Protestantism they were rejecting. Still, they were in the habit of living with "Bibles" and finding themselves in the plot. And even while some countercultural movements assaulted traditional understandings with their new texts, other factions in the United States would promote the Bible itself as having light to throw on America. President Ronald Reagan liked to ask Americans to turn to 2 Chronicles 7:14 and see themselves in it: "If my people who are called by my name humble themselves, pray, seek my face, and turn from their wicked ways, then I will hear from heaven, and will forgive their sin and heal their land."

Invoking this was a very Protestant thing to do. Can one picture a political leader in Italy or Spain, the Netherlands or Ireland, going directly to the language and stipulations of God's scriptured covenant with Israel as they would set out to manage, control, and direct a people who, Protestant or not, were to follow?

Of the sixth element I am least confident: the survival of grace in the *creencias* of America beyond Protestantism (and as we saw before, within Protestantism). I heard Dean Alan Jones of Grace Cathedral in San Francisco drop a homiletic line that was apt: "We are a society in which everything is permitted, and nothing is forgiven." To the degree that that observation is in place—I believe it to be broadly accurate—it is a reversal of the Protestant witness. That witness concentrated on a God whose mandates were to be taken with utter seriousness, as Jesus took them and transmitted them, while heightening them in the text that has come to us as the Sermon on the Mount, a God who then would forgive miscreants who repented. Instead, anything goes until the investigative journalists tell much or the *"Mommy Dearest"* autobiographers tell all, at which point no one is forgiven.

Or this element is compromised in a culture where the proclamation of grace in church or in society comes in the form that Dietrich Bonhoeffer called "cheap grace." Yale's Lutheran theologian Paul Holmer said he would visit Lutheran churches where the "pure Lutheran-Pauline gospel" was being preached. Yes, the sermons were orthodox. The minister would say to the congregation that because grace prevailed, they should *not* seek to gain God's favor through their merits; they should not try to get there by their works, their strivings. Holmer would survey the dozing, complacent congregation, and ask, "Who's trying?"

Still something of a forgiving and being forgiven spirit

sometimes operates on the national level: in repentances, cheap as many of them may be, over slavery, over policies that glossed over abuse. I could find more illustrations, but they tend to verge on cheap grace, which is not grace in the old-Protestant sense, so I will make least of this item and move on to the next.

The seventh element of much Protestant teaching and example when it ran the show is the emphasis on *agency*. Double predestination did not stand a chance in the American ethos because the same preachers who preached it then called for listeners to make the Evangelical decision to be converts, to be doers in society.

Dissertation writer and former student James Block showed me not only how this agentic strand came to America from English and other philosophy but also how it came to be characteristic of Protestant witness. Certainly, some colonists and immigrants came as persecutees who were *seeking* freedom, but most of them—serfs, indentured servants, the poor of Europe and Asia (African slaves weren't asked)—came to be agents, to better themselves, to reshape an environment. To do that, they *needed* freedom.

One can learn to be an agent and to promote agency without a Protestant cleric preaching the notion and inspiring the impulse; Block traces much of the emphasis on agency to Hobbes and other rather strikingly non-Protestant philosophers. But most visitors to America in the Protestant prime, Alexis de Tocqueville in the 1830s being a good example, stressed how the churches were proclaiming, nurturing, and organizing to promote agency. Freedom and grace were divine gifts, but those gifts had to be worked through humans as agents, just as God's gifts had to be worked through humans in the process of nation-building.

The final *creencia* is a cluster centered around biblical themes witnessed to and deposited by Protestants and diffused into the culture at large so much so that such themes no longer need Protestants to do the promoting.

Some years ago Paul Pribbenow, a University of Chicago dissertation writer and now president of Rockford College, wanted to see what elements of the biblical and Protestant credos might nurture people in professions invented in the twentieth century: social work (his field then), fund-raising (into which he went at first for employment), and public relations.

He proposed three. First among these, at least first for me, is *mission*. Americans write mission statements and determine to live by them, to be judged by them, or to be exposed as hypocrites when others examine them. Individuals are asked to define their mission in life. The nation as a whole is to have a mission, whether as God's agent against "evil empires" in wars, as a rebuilder after destruction (e.g., the Marshall Plan in Europe and the MacArthur policies in Japan after World War II), or as a sometimes generous humanitarian in foreign policy. (I won't go into *how* generous the United States has been; it ranks relatively low among nations in terms of the proportion of GNP used for policy expenditures on humanitarianism, but individuals "as Americans" often support voluntary causes as part of the national mission.) The national mission, and Protestant biblical interpretation, furthermore, can be traced even to Manifest Destiny.

Another motif is *stewardship.* Tempering some of the Protestant free-enterprise rhetoric and ethos is the notion that in the competitive scramble for acquisition people should reflect on how natural resources and the products derived from them, along with all possessions, are "on loan." Citizens are to be stewards. Much of the discourse about saving the environment relates to the old language of stewardship, though admittedly a mix of philosophies and poetics (Eastern, Native American, transcendentalist, and the like) have harmonically converged with this one aspect of the late-Protestant witness.

Another motif is *vocation.* In historic Protestantism, vocation meant a response of laity and clergy alike to divine mandates. In the Middle Ages, says the broad-brush painting historian, vocation was for monks and nuns and priests. Once the Reformation took hold, all the baptized were to find their divine calling, whether as merchants and lawyers, peasants or diaper washers. They were "called." Many scholars traced this notion as being integral to the Protestant ethic, which, in turn, became secularized. Even people who do not recognize the caller as God are to pursue a responsible "calling" or "vocation."

Vigencias: Protestant Binding Customs

Ortega linked *creencias* to *vigencias,* which may be roughly described as the "binding customs" of a culture. These tend to be unwritten. If I do not bribe the customs agents in one national culture, I will not get my bags in any hurry, if at all. If I bribe them in another, I will be detained. The laws of the land do not spell this out. My guidebook is not likely to put risky advice about how to get along, in bold print, for legal reasons. But somehow I must learn that "that is how we do things here" or "that isn't done around here." If I want to do business with one company and I slip money surreptitiously to a bribee, all will be well. If I try that in another company, I will be shown to the door. "That is how we do things here" in the first instance; "that isn't done around here" in the other.

Protestants in the midst of pluralism and its aftermath wrestle, just as Protestants in their prime wrestled, with ill-defined *vigencias.* What I call the enactments of freedom, the ways Americans act on, or interpret how to act on, the principles contained in the founding documents that have assured freedom, are a prime example. A most obvious application for the religious is in the debates over the First Amendment's clauses forbidding religious establishment and against prohibiting the free exercise of religion. Both sides on all the issues use the same rule book, the U.S. Constitution, including the first ten amendments: those who advocate and those who oppose school vouchers that may be used in parochial schools;

those who are for gun control and those who argue for freer access to arms; those who are pro rights of the accused and those who see criminals wherever there are allegations. All make their appeal "scripturally" to that same slim document and long tradition of interpretation.

Both insist that they are advocating freedom, but they are asking, Whose freedom? Whose authorization? Whose protection? To insist that only Protestants ask such questions or that Protestants were the only agents when the laws behind the binding customs celebrating freedom were enacted would be bizarre. But clearly their forms of biblical witness were main contributors, along with what Protestants derived from the Enlightenment and what those Protestants had to do in practical situations. When Americans come across nations and cultures that have little concern for rights or that have more concern for tribal and communal rights than for individual ones, they often express bemusement: How can that other culture fail to see the benefits of what is done around here?

Another element of the binding customs relates to the contribution of the Enlightenment, alluded to in the previous paragraph, insofar as the act of living with both Protestant-preached biblical themes and eighteenth-century (Protestant?) Enlightenment "doctrines" has led citizens to live with practical ambiguities. My teacher Sidney E. Mead liked to show how incompatible, both logically and theologically, were the particularist interpretations of freedom that Protestant biblicists promoted on one hand and the universalist Enlightenment ideology on the other (though I would contend that the Enlightenment ideology was also particularist, simply particularist in a different way). The Protestant interpretation found freedom in Christ through revelation in the Bible. The Enlightenment ideology found freedom in Nature's God and Nature's Law apart from and not needing particular revelation, such as in the form of biblical witness.

Mead thought that Protestant Americans could not digest the Enlightenment or what he called the (non-Protestant) "Religion of the Republic" but were unwilling to regurgitate the practices *(vigencias?)* that connected with and derived from it. What is striking is how undisturbed most citizens are by this anomaly, even when it is called to their attention. I think of Will Herberg as sociologist saying that every complex society needs a "civic faith," an integrating civil religion, and that America had one, and it was generally creative and benign. And then I think of Will Herberg as theologian, devoted to the Torah and the covenant and the God of Israel, saying that such civic faiths *had* by definition to be idolatrous and that idolatry was the first sin in the eyes of God as revealed in scripture.

On one hand, theologically, many of the Protestant heritage say that salvation comes only to those who in faith acknowledge Christ. Then, asked to look around at their "good" compatriots, they often blithely—and one might say from the civil angle, creatively—drop the "only" and see everyone "in different boats heading for the same shore."

A third component of the *vigencias,* the binding customs, is the competitive dimension. Protestant support of the free market did not come all at once. The New England Puritans developed and wanted to live by and within a controlled economy. They would live as any medieval Thomist would with prescriptions for "fair price" and "just wage." They were dragged screaming, often by competition from folks like the Baptists down the shore in Newport, Rhode Island, to forget about such notions and take the free-enterprise plunge. Early in the nineteenth century father Lyman Beecher preached static status: The poor should live with godly contentment; the rich should know the divine burden placed on the rich. A generation later, his son Henry Ward Beecher, pulling at other Protestant strands, saw poverty as God's punishment for those who lacked ambition or energy. To be poor was a vice; to be rich was a blessing.

If the consequence of these messages was again ambivalence, Protestant America could live with that. The preachers could preach salvation as a gift, citing the writings of the apostle Paul, and then quote the same biblical writer to say that followers should "work out their own salvation" and, pursuing an athletic metaphor, "earn" the reward by having run well. Sebastian de Grazia in a book on *Anomie* suggested that anomie, normless apathy, could result when young people were given constant and conflicting messages: "Compete" and "Cooperate." Anything on the right side of the law and sometimes beyond it was appropriate for competitors. Just ask the robber barons and their pastors, who saw the plundering, successful competitors endow churchly causes. Yet in churches and service clubs and in the binding customs of the country, equally strong messages said, "Cooperate."

The corollary of this competitive principle, so vivid in church life, had to do with denominationalism and ecumenism. The churches all confessed faith in "one, holy, catholic, and apostolic church" and were happy to put energies into the demonstrably positive effects on church growth if they motivated competition among the congregations and the denominations. The secular counterpart fuses the competitive principle with the free-market economy, adhered to by citizens far from any direct Protestant lineage.

This list of ambiguities, which were built into the Protestant deposit in the culture and which endure even now when the Protestant witness is muffled and diffused, rather than clearly demarcated, could be extended. But the observation that what is or isn't done around here, in the national culture, relates in complex ways to what Protestants did when they ran the show and to what they have done since in a pluralistic society.

Phases in Running the Show

Protestantism in its broadest frame and ambition did not run the show in a single, static pattern from 1607 to 1955. How it came to its place, how it held that place, and then how it shared (or lost) that place is a complex drama. Paying attention to the stages or acts helps make clear what managing, controlling, and directing might mean.

To conceive now of how there would have seemed to be little chance of the northern part of the Western Hemisphere becoming Protestant on the eve of its discovery is difficult. However, until the Muslim forces were beat back from Spain in 1492, they looked poised to become the explorers of the Atlantic. Having conquered Constantinople forty years earlier, they were moving toward Vienna and were threatening to turn the Mediterranean into a Muslim lake. But after the armies of Ferdinand and Isabella in Spain defeated them, they retreated and were not in a position to explore. Otherwise, picture a mosque where Old First Church is.

Furthermore, in 1492 Catholicism was the religion of destiny. Protestantism could not have been an American force because there was no Protestantism. Protest movements in many places in Europe would not occur until the early sixteenth century, and even then Protestantism did not have its almost accidentally acquired name until 1529. After the Reformation, the Protestantized parts of the waning Holy Roman Empire and France, Protestant Netherlands, and sometimes Protestant England were ready to go, but they waited until the century ended before they started the move west.

By 1607 England, at least, was hungry for exploration, expansion, and opportunities for settlement in and commerce with the western shores of the Atlantic. And come the Protestants did, from Sweden and the Netherlands, some from

Germany, a larger number from Huguenot France, but mainly from England. By the end of the colonial period Catholic Maryland was no longer Catholic, and not a single Catholic church existed in New England. Catholics were prominent only in the New France that was part of Canada. In the English colonies, Catholics were confined to Maryland and southern Pennsylvania. Perhaps there were thirty thousand of them by the end of the colonial period. The three thousand Jews were not in a position to run the show. Native Americans and African Americans, the slaves, stood no chance. Colonial definition in respect to religion was, simply, Protestant of a sort that paid respect to the Hebrew Scriptures, but which hardly knew living Jews.

The second, or national, period began with the War of Independence and the drafting of the Constitution and lasted until the mid–nineteenth century. During this time, religious authorities linked with Enlightenment figures to form odd couples: Baptist elder John Leland with Thomas Jefferson in Virginia, Calvinist evangelist George Whitefield with Benjamin Franklin in Pennsylvania. Such men were the main agencies for shaping *creencias* and establishing precedents in respect to the *vigencias* of the day. Postmillennialism inspired efforts of mission and mercy. Lay leaders formed voluntary associations, while evangelizers went out to win the West.

The Protestant national period was challenged as Catholic immigrants arrived from Ireland, Germany, and elsewhere. Protestant Americans did what they could to thwart the efforts of Catholics to win America. What has come down to us as the Protestant Crusade began. Protestants were quite ecumenical in their outreach, but the new Mormon group and the old Catholic group were not to share in the shaping.

In literary circles other voices gradually came to be heard. Nathaniel Hawthorne and Herman Melville reworked the biblical myths cherished in Protestantism, while Ralph Waldo Emerson and Henry David Thoreau, among others, extricated themselves from the same mythic framework and, except in their individualism, did not look very Protestant to most readers then or later. Arguments supporting slavery or making the case for abolition were profoundly rooted in Protestant biblical themes. There was no churchly presence to challenge the Protestant running.

In the third, or later national, period, from mid–nineteenth century through the Civil War and its aftermath, the rise of industrial and corporate America, and new immigrations, Protestantism still lead the spiritual forces in determining what was in the show and who was to run it. Movements that scholars associate with secularization grew apace, but Protestantism continued to prosper in the Gilded Age and during the growth of great cities. Ominously, in the eyes of Protestant shapers and movers, the number of Jewish immigrants grew rapidly after 1881, following pogroms in Eastern Europe, but Jews were still largely off to themselves in a few cities like New York. Catholics, who began to come in large numbers after 1830 and continued to come through the Irish potato famines of the late 1840s and all through the second half of the century, served more to unite Protestants against them than to replace them as cultural arbiters. Even though immigration did not slow until after the Exclusion Act of 1924, non-Protestants did not have sufficient money, education, or social location to determine much of life and thought and practice beyond their own subcultures.

The fourth period, commencing in the 1930s, marked the prospering of religious groups called Fundamentalist and conservative, while the mainline began to show signs of decline. World War II and the return of service people taught in Protestant Sunday schools, however, gave mainline Protestantism one more chance in northern metropolitan areas. The move by mainly rural southern blacks to northern cities led to growth in African American churches, and though they could do little to make their case in the larger culture, they left their stamp on black culture and kept most of African Americans Protestant. Back-to-Africa nationalist movements and the budding Islamic groups were statistically too small to have much sway.

By 1955 and the start of the fifth period, however, this was all ready to change. Catholics, benefiting from the GI Bill, flocked to and graduated from universities into the middle class and positions of influence. Jews, enjoying their new situation as partners in the new invention, the Judeo-Christian tradition, were poised for new opportunities. It would be one of their own, Will Herberg, who showed special insight into emergent post-Protestant America (in which Protestants would remain clustered as the largest group by far).

Managing, Controlling, Directing in These Phases

During the colonial era, in which nine of thirteen colonies enjoyed or endured Protestant establishments, noticing how the privileged Protestants ran the show religiously and in no small measure culturally is not difficult. Running the show is what establishment, state support, fiscal subsidy, and honoring are all about.

Signs that the nation that would emerge from the colonies would not be a permanent Protestantdom, however, were apparent from the beginning, as from the start one form of Protestantism gave place to other forms and sometimes to other forms of religion and ways of thought. In 1654 domain-seeking Dutch Reformed Peter Stuyvesant wanted to privilege the Reformed Church. But for commercial reasons and because of the will of his Dutch West Indies sponsors, he had to make room for Jews and behind them, Lutherans and Mennonists and Catholics.

In New England, soon enough, as historian Richard Bushman puts it, Puritans turned Yankee, dropping their otherworldly or world-denying predilections for an at first grudging and then enthusiastic embrace of the Yankee-merchant secular way. How did this happen? First, the inherited way was inconveniencing and embarrassing. The Puritans had a controlled economy in which they set "fair prices" on a kind of natural law ground. They would say that a purveyor should sell a product for what would be a fair price if there were no shortage. Then came a shortage of nails, and hardware man Robert Keayne raised prices. Reaction against his violation, which amounted to nothing more than capitalism in action, was violent. He had to make a long apology, *The Apologia of Robert Keayne,* in order to retain church membership and citizenship rights. A colony could not force that kind of response very often without losing credibility.

A second way has to do with competition and survivability. Massachusetts Bay did all that it could to keep outside influences away. When merchant ships came into the harbor, restrictions often kept crews from coming ashore and potentially tainting the city of Boston with their alien ways. Not many sea miles away was Newport, the harbor in the colony of Rhode Island, founded by Baptists, who did not impose such restrictions and who welcomed diversity and outside influences. Boston merchants, seeing the trade move to Newport, found ways to adjust so that they could compete in what was becoming a rather worldly Yankee society. The churches in Massachusetts did not wither and die—they were even to experience some religious awakenings—but they could not remain too legalistic, too self-enclosed in their older Puritan styles. The majority of the citizens were still Protestant, but there was ever less of a ——dom, less of a domain.

In the South, Baptists from New England displaced the

establishment. Other newcomers from Europe had no love for Anglicanism, and the sons and daughters of Anglican southern colonists who got heated up by evangelists and awakeners changed the direction of their loyalties. Methodists joined with Baptists to put Episcopalians on the defensive in their own territory.

In the Enlightenment, Protestant motifs had to yield to rationalist themes and forms of expression. The First Amendment doomed church establishment in the states. Such establishment ended in Massachusetts as it had ended in all the other colonies-turned-states by 1833. What some called a second establishment resulted. This one ruled not by law but in the ethos, not by coercion but by persuasion, not by privilege but through voluntary assent. Of course, vestigial establishments, churches of privilege, still existed. College-bred people, mainly men, of mainstream Protestant extraction were the elites in the North. But they had less weight to throw around in the South, with its masses of Baptist, Methodists, and then Disciples. Still, we might say that in this period many Protestants recovered in ethos what they had lost in law.

Two unifiers helped the Protestants look stronger than they were. A few "infidels," freethinkers, often European-derived communitarian experimenters who gained reputations as sexual libertarians and economic subversives, provided all Protestant parties with an often imagined but seldom real threat to ally against. The other unifier was the fight against Catholicism. Though few dead bodies—yes, there were some!—accrued in the Protestant-Catholic conflict, Catholics were still limited in their ability to shape the culture beyond their own bounds.

Catholicism served to unite the strands of Protestantism until almost 1955. Near the middle of the twentieth century a group called Protestants and Other Americans United for Separation of Church and State became a watchdog on the church-state front, but it is remembered most for its strident warnings about and strategies against Catholics. Protestants found anti-Catholicism a form of respectable prejudice.

Protestantism suffered numerous jolts while it was still uniting against infidels and papists. First were different styles of influence on differing cultures east along the coast and west, west of the mountains and out into the vast West. Worse was the splitting along North/South lines before, during, and after the Civil War. Baptist, Presbyterian, and Methodist bodies, each of which had strong influence on its region and its pro- or antisecession faction, formed separate and rival jurisdictions, and Protestants could not run the show nationally because for four years of war there were in feel, if not in recognized constitutionalism, two nations.

A third sundering occurred as new theologies, liberalisms versus conservatisms, biblical critics versus critics of critics, took hold in the late nineteenth century, and Protestantism ventured toward the point of schism as Fundamentalist/modernist camps became permanent in the 1920s. The *Scopes* trial and its effects in Tennessee around 1925 left one side of the

Protestant nation affirming the losing proevolution thrust after the court case and the other side negating it militantly.

The "voluntary church" nurtured the rise of an "errand of mercy." In it lay people and some clerics in various bodies, but almost independent of those bodies, formed reform and charitable agencies. This "errand" effected an almost unimaginable cultural stamp. Lay members of the Protestant churches found new cultural slots, and they had to be reckoned with, especially when they fired not at secularists or Catholics but at fellow Protestants with whom each disagreed. Intra-Protestant division over abolition and similar causes resulted.

To take this quick-paced, satellite-distanced view allows us to see who was *not* included in the Protestants-who-ran-the-show company. Women, first of all. They probably outnumbered the men in the church pews, but they had few professional slots open to them, were being ordained to clergy almost nowhere, and did not get to set the agenda. Second, the poets, almost a code word for post-Protestant transcendentalists. They drew their inspiration not from Calvin or Jesus but from nature, the Greeks and Romans, and Eastern religion. Some were called "Yankee Hindoos." Third, much of the nation's corporate leadership. Such leaders had grown autonomous and exerted power with no special recourse to Protestant ethical lineages.

In elite culture, privilege remained. There were very, *very* few Jews and Catholics in registers like *Who's Who*. In all but Catholic colleges, prior to the GI bill after World War II, the overwhelming population statistics were on the Protestant side, and anti-Jewish quotas at Ivy League schools continued to exist even after World War II. Native Americans, African Americans in segregation, and Asian Americans, who were suspect and sequestered in West Coast cities, ruled their own culture but could do little about the larger one.

Managing, controlling, and directing, however weakly or strongly, remained largely a Protestant enterprise, if we want to measure influence beyond religious subcultures. André Siegfried's and H. Richard Niebuhr's Protestant America was *not* to see fewer Protestants as a percentage of the population. Most of Protestantism's churches and ventures proceeded as before. But after 1955, they were not to run the show. They could live off and contribute to the *creencias* and *vigencias* of the nation, but they could not dominate or be isolated in respect to other forces and creeds.

MORE RINGS IN
THE CIRCUS

Realized Pluralism, after 1955

T HE METAPHOR OF AMERICAN RELIGION as a show is
not meant to demean ventures involving the sacred, life and
death and eternity, and ethics. Instead the metaphor is in-
tended to suggest that under the big tent of American life, the
question of who runs the show, who manages, controls, and
directs it, always endures. Though American religions have always had a significant, almost incomprehensibly complex diversity, even well before the first Europeans came, after they
arrived, the force of numbers and influence and the dispropor-
tionate access to instruments of power gave a broad spectrum
of Protestants the advantage in reaching the larger nation's
ear and heart and mind, to say nothing of its pocketbook and
law book.

After the mid–twentieth century, however, long quiescent and quiet, often suppressed, voices gained a hearing. This new situation, still under the one large sacred canopy, featured more rings than one, more subshows than one, more managers, controllers, and directors, and more managed, controlled, and directed people and forces than had been visible earlier. This change did not mean the end of all power for those who had earlier run the show. Rather, this change meant that those who had run the show had to share power and spotlight with others, often at the expense of their own role and voice.

In the first chapter I marked the turn of a very complex, decades-long process with reference to one book, Will Herberg's *Protestant-Catholic-Jew* in 1955. We need to revisit that book now to get some perspective on the move by Americans to recognize pluralism as never before.

The Jewish sociologist-theologian Herberg observed many changes after World War II. These included the move of Jews from inner-city ghettos to the blended populations of the suburbs and to other situations that were costly to the identity of people and peoples, an erosion of identity that people experienced as a threat. How were they to retain, retrieve, or manufacture identity? Herberg drew on a thesis about immigration, one that contended that "what the son wants to forget, the grandson wants to remember." Immigrants retain the old ways; their children reject many of them; their grandchildren are lost, confused, subject to anomie.

Members of the third generation cannot go back to retrieve

the language of the old country. Certainly, they may adopt elements from it that we might call aesthetic, decorlike—for example, patronizing restaurants of an ethnic character or revisiting the old cookbooks—but nothing serves them better than some version of the religions of their ancestors. They identify with these, whether they practice the faith or not.

And so a revival of religion occurred in the Eisenhower era. The revival was not profound in Herberg's reckoning and in the eyes of many other observers. It was not ethically rich, not inconveniencing. In fact, it was *conveniencing*. And though people identified themselves as Protestant or Catholic or Jew, they also found themselves becoming devoted to a homogenizing civic faith, a religion of the American Way of Life.

Herberg paid little attention to African Americans, Hispanics, Asians, women, Fundamentalists, Evangelicals, Mormons, Eastern Orthodox, or "sects and cults," the marginalized. His citizens mostly converged on three rather conventional pools. Herberg saw his nation diversely enough, however, that America came to be regarded not as Protestant or Christian but as Judeo-Christian. Campus Christian observances, including those at state universities, became Religious Emphasis Weeks, to which tireless priests, ministers, and rabbis migrated to assess the role of American religion. The fact that a Jew, not a white Anglo-Saxon Protestant (or WASP, a coinage of this era) wrote the book was significant. That many readers were Catholics, newly welcomed in tax-based public colleges and universities, was another sign of a new day.

The next twelve or thirteen years saw impressive enlargements of Herberg's trifaith picture. He had hardly mentioned the Holocaust or the 1948 birth of Israel. The war in Israel in 1967 led American Jews to reappraise their situation, and new articulations of Judaism emerged. The civil rights and black power movements, both with their roots and corollaries in African American churches, further changed the mix. Native American, Hispanic American, women's liberation, and gay and lesbian movements enriched the picture.

A new Evangelicalism rose as a challenger to historic Protestantism. The old eastern citadels of Protestantism faced a variety of people with what might be called country and western styles of religion, rising in the South and West. (Such Evangelicals had always been there, but the whole nation now had to acknowledge them.)

In intellectual life, white and secularized Protestants had dominated. Now academics, writers, dramatists, artists, and musicians as likely as not were Jewish, African American, Catholic, or something else further. Hollywood films (mainly produced by Jews) from the 1920s into the 1950s rarely took up racial or ethnic themes; that, too, changed.

America as such and as a whole, it turned out, was too hot for the mitt-sized glove of white Protestantism to hold everything. Along the way came a shift in the *creencias* and *vigencias,* and Protestants of the older style adapted. Thus, through the 1940s many of them favored school prayer in a kind of generalized liberal Protestant style fused with elements of inoffensive humanisms (they criticized secular humanism). Now, after Supreme Court decisions ruled school prayer unconstitutional, most of them went along, leaving the attempt to keep vestiges of Protestant hegemony, call it now Evangelicaldom, in schools and public places.

The school-prayer decisions of the U.S. Supreme Court in 1962 and 1963 were major elements in the change of the cultural landscape. In 1965, while the nation was watching the Vietnam War, the civil rights movement, and Great Society legislation unfold, few noticed as Congress approved changes in immigration law that effectively altered the covenant imposed in 1924, one that had favored white Protestant populations. These changes made it possible for non-Protestants to arrive from Asia and Hispanic America.

World War II and its aftereffects were significant in the switch from Protestant-run to pluralist America. Though racial integration in the armed forces developed slowly, the roles played by nonwhites and non-Protestants were newly recognized. Wartime symbolisms favored themes such as that of the four chaplains of three faiths who stayed with their ship and went down with their men. Films about the military typically featured platoons or bomber squadrons with a chaplain of each faith. Brotherhood Week and interfaith efforts by the National Conference of Christians and Jews came into vogue. The election of John F. Kennedy in 1960 meant the end of Protestant bloc politics against Catholics. Protestants and Other Americans United for Separation of Church and State, to the degree that it was perceived as anti-Catholic, progressively lost favor. Catholics were on the move: Bishop Fulton Sheen was one of the two most popular religious figures on television, the other being Evangelical Billy Graham. Celebrated converts such as playwright Claire Booth Luce led non-Catholics to have to reckon with new company among elites.

At midcentury *Christian Century* magazine was among the instruments of change. A cover feature, "Pluralism, a National Menace" (critical of a Buffalo bishop who wanted tax funds for parochial schools), was among the first of the entries in a new category, Pluralism, in the *Readers' Guide to Periodical Literature.* The term had rarely appeared in similar guides in previous decades. Jewish scholar and advocate Horace M. Kallen had talked favorably about cultural pluralism earlier, but not much came of it. Now, observers of all faiths and no faith began to contend over the word.

I usually define this pluralism of a sort that can only exist in a republic and that must exist, if the republic is to be sound and dynamic, in athletic terms. First, any number (here, of religions and ethnic groups) can play. Second, great numbers do. Third, the players must accede to some rules, in this case condensed in the First Amendment religion clause. In addition, an ethos—a set of practices, a cluster of *vigencias*—reinforce the pluralism. Brotherhood Week, trifaith prayers at presidential inaugurations, criticism of proselytism, invention of interfaith dialogue: These are all samples.

The Consultation on Church Union, an effort to bring into

concord the mainline Protestant denominations, was enriched, then slowed and altered, as it came to include African American churches. African Americans did not want to be integrated into what was but rather to change what was, and they did. More dramatic were the rise of the Nation of Islam—black Muslims—and the presence in some African American Christian churches of a black Madonna. Soon, largely white Protestant congregations were singing spirituals and gospel and soul music, much of it far from the cultural legacy of the old WASP liturgical and musical traditions.

The women's movement worked two ways to undercut the hold of white Protestant men. First, it was transdenominational, interfaith, and often blended religious motifs with secular feminist ones. Being women, fighting for women's rights, and offering understandings of their life as women were activities that often defined women more than being Presbyterian or Lutheran. Second, within the groups, women revisited and reinterpreted texts that they saw as having favored patriarchy (in the managing, controlling, and directing of things). For the old patriarchies to survive unreformed would have been difficult.

Another element in the realization of pluralism was the new ecumenism that resulted from Vatican II. It was no longer possible for Protestantism to define itself as non- or anti-Catholic, when so many Catholics and Protestants found common cause in social action, citizenship, voluntary associations, biblical and theological studies, devotional life, and ministry. After the final session of the Council in 1965, at which the Catholic Church changed its teaching on religion in republics, old attacks on Catholicism no longer made sense and certainly were not fair.

As already implied, the bonding of religion with ethnicity brought realized pluralism as ethnic identities came to serve as definers for millions of citizens. The Pentagon of hyphenated ethnicities, written of by David Hollinger in *Postethnic America*, European-, Native-, African-, Asian-, and Hispanic-American, included highly diverse elements, even sometimes within themselves, and these ethnicities, in turn, had to be taken into consideration in everything from political campaigns to marketing. Many of these included non- and anti-Protestant constituencies.

During the period after 1955 the virtual schism between mainline Protestants and those in the Evangelical-Fundamentalist-Pentecostal-conservative cohort made it ever more difficult for Protestantism as such to run the show. Did one turn to Union Theological Seminary in New York or to Billy Graham, who seemed to be everywhere, for interpreting American life "under God"? Did one line up with the liberal National Council of Churches or the conservative National Association of Evangelicals? The invention of televangelism produced or made possible the rise of a new breed of celebrities, all of them Evangelical, but none of them identified through Evangelicalism with Protestantism or as Protestants.

To arrive at this point in the chapter with only slight men-

tion of the sixties suggests not a lack of interest in the pluralist upheavals of that decade but instead how much occurred
before and apart from its tumults to redefine America and
its religion. The sixties brought a radicalization of religious
groups and movements, among many secular forces and parties. The left challenged liberal Protestantism with radicals
who saw it as too concessive to the old order, an order that had
to be brought down. Spiritual experimentalists—Jesus people
movements, users of psychedelic drugs for spiritual highs,
devotees of liturgies featuring rock and other new music—
forced the publics to take refuge in dwindling mainline Protestantism or to leave its ranks because it seemed too adapted,
too boring: unserviceable.

Political activity among Evangelicals, who had long been
perceived as passive, otherworldly, rose to the attention of the
nation beginning around 1964 with the Goldwater campaign.
In what later became the Moral Majority and Christian Coalition movements, Evangelicals manifested their desire to run
the show, to manage and control and direct, pointedly in criticism of and as an alternative to mainline Protestantism.

Finally, later in the period, people spoke not only of post-
Protestant but also of postmodern America. A new eclecti-
cism, a take-your-pick spirituality, worked against traditional,
inherited, multigenerational groupings.

Each of these observations could well merit book-length
attention, and whole books exist on each. Here I use them simply as pointers, for reminders that Protestant-run religious

America was no longer that. These changes have evoked many analyses and interpretations about the changed character of religion in public life, including such typical items as the following:

First, in matters of power and influence, pluralist America saw more emphasis placed on the individual achievement of religious leaders than on a leader's ascription to particular religious views. Everyone knew Martin Luther King Jr., pastor of one small church and then leader of a voluntary organization, but who knew the names of the presidents of the various African American denominations? Many Catholics focused more on the opinions of theologians like Hans Küng, Rosemary Ruether, or John Courtney Murray than on the signals of their church-appointed bishop. "Death of God" or "secular" theologians like Harvey Cox and social activists like William Sloane Coffin were recognized in the public realm more than were elected leaders of various denominations. The publics were busy spotting celebrities, each of whom created his or her own constituency, more than paying attention to the custodians of traditions, including the Protestant one. Certainly, Protestants were in the mix of influentials, but they were there as individuals, not because they were bishops or moderators or presidents of denominations.

This change led to a second adjustment, one of a psychological sort. Though the politics of nostalgia had its place among Protestants, mainline leaders and followers spent far less energy using it than did Evangelicals, who started movements to "Retake America." Florida conservative pastor James Kennedy of Coral Ridge was among the leaders of such movements. Though many of these movements were open to Catholics and others, most of them were out to create a kind of Evangelicaldom. Many were originally moved by what I call "politics of resentment"—a belief that they had been slighted or demeaned—but they turned quickly to a politics of "will to power." From the election of Ronald Reagan to their virtual control of the Republican Party's choices and decisions in the second Bush administration, they tasted enough success to aspire to run not just a party but the nation.

Significantly, the counterforces were not liberal Protestant, or at least not liberal Protestant in isolation. Groups with more liberal agendas, such as People for the American Way, tended to include Jews, Catholics, and people of secular mentality at least as much as they included Protestants.

A third feature of post-Protestant pluralist life was the appearance of people who, religiously, matched the description of what psychiatrist Robert J. Lifton called "Protean" in his book *Boundaries*. Just as the god Proteus could change appearance and behavior, Protean men and women could attach themselves to an endless array of often contradictory leaders and texts. Religions came to have a kind of cafeteria-line character. In that line older styles of Protestantism, even when adapted, looked conventional, while the seekers were looking for the exotic and esoteric.

Against the Protean religious personality Lifton posed the

"constrictive" religious personality. Seeking identity or fearing the loss of one, people with a preference for the constrictive turned to fundamentalisms or new religious movements that screened out all but one set of signals, those posed by a leader. Such a leader could be a local pastor serving as a biblical interpreter or the founder of what for a time was called a "cult." By definition, most kinds of non-Fundamentalist Protestantism resisted such kinds of enclosure and had to yield many of their offspring to groups that would constrict options. A mainline Protestant's daughter, for example, might have found herself rooming with a member of an intense conversion-minded group on campus and then turned to the group because her familial patterns had looked too nonintense.

To explore all the ramifications of the turn to pluralism is tempting. For example, in the course of the 1970s its cultural dimensions came to the fore in the largely academic movement of multiculturalism. This movement often focused on the life of ethnic, religious, racial, class, gendered, or taste-based subcultures, as they bade for attention, often in isolation or in contrasting postures (e.g., in contrast with Dead White European Males and their American analogs). This movement, of course, shows that Protestants learned to share space and power, a point that has already been explored.

Perhaps the most dramatic point to make is one so taken for granted that it goes virtually unobserved: this transition, this power shift, occurred with no "dead bodies," no fundamental shift in polity. There were and are what came to be called Culture Wars, but the battle lines have not been drawn on Protestant-versus-Others lines so much as they have been drawn from within Protestantism and in alliance with criss-crossing factions from other groups.

The fact that this was so bloodless, so often unnoticed, has to do with many factors. One of them was the polity itself, the kind of republic invented by Protestants in coalition with (semi-Protestant?) Enlightenment leaders. While they may have been people with the normal prejudices belonging to most human individuals and groups, they initiated philoso-phies that muted their potentially lethal rhetoric of particu-larity.

The crisscrossing effect, mentioned earlier, played its part. Protestants could have aimed to remove Catholic and Jewish voices from the culture, but if successful, alienating such potential allies would have simply provided a larger body for unlike-minded thinkers to draw from to create their own coun-tercultural (counter-Protestant) movement. We could ask, "If you, representing your group (whether on left or right or in the center), wanted to shoot, at whom would you point your gun?" American life is characterized by many kinds of cleav-ages that could induce conflict. For example, class dictates in no small measure where one lives and with whom one affiliates. But an anti-Catholic or anti-Jewish Protestant laborer would likely be shooting at and, if successful in killing, losing an ally or a potential ally in the movement to reorganize labor.

Pluralism is no magic cure. It lacks a clear philosophical

base. Adhering to its principles and ethos will not save souls, make sad hearts glad, or bring comfort to the dying. It is an attempt to find a "least worst" solution to sharing a polity, an attempt to meet the challenges involved when so many voices are in competition.

Father John Courtney Murray in his book *We Hold These Truths* posed a fundamental problem with pluralism when he confessed that it was "against the will of God" but "was the human condition." Such a statement leaves questions: Will all agree that religious pluralism is against the will of God? Are those who accept pluralism as the "human condition" observing something that is against the will of God? Murray worried: In a republic, when people disagree over profound issues, can they address these if they lack some sort of *consensus juris* grounded in a philosophy of some sort, in metaphysics or theology?

So diverse and divided is America today that the metaphor of the tent may no longer be applicable. So we have to ask, Is there still a tent?

IS THERE STILL A TENT, OR ARE THERE MANY TENTS?

Protestantism Gone Public, within Pluralism

A̳s shown previously, Protestantism was a major element of—and no doubt on spiritual levels the chief contribu-
tor to—many of the *creencias* and *vigencias* in American culture. After having held a privileged position from 1607 to
1955 the many forms of Protestantism began to yield their
place and share it with non-Protestant contributors, challengers, and rivals. Where, then, is the place of Protestantism(s) in
emergent America? There are many discourses on pluralism,
of course, but not many take up directly the interplay of Protestant forces or influences and the complex of "realized pluralism."

Several profound crises in American life have made the
question of how these two interplay more intense. The public

responses to the terrorist attacks on September 11, 2001, illustrate the changes. Like most nations in crisis, America knew it had to be united. Unity implied communication between religious groups. This was the problem. Whereas a half century earlier Americans of different faiths would have headed for their own particular sanctuaries and let Protestant clerics lead public gatherings, America was different now.

The presence of an imam, a rabbi, Eastern Orthodox and Roman Catholic clerics, among others, at the side of the president of the United States, Protestant evangelist Billy Graham, and other Protestants, embodied the pluralist state. At an observance at Yankee Stadium a few days later, the gathering—for a moment at least—of several religious groups to mourn and to demonstrate a new set of resolves, placed an even greater emphasis on religious diversity. In thousands of local communities something similar was occurring.

Most evident was the mixture of curiosity, suspicion, and hope shown Muslims by non-Muslims. In any local community a lecture by a Muslim would draw capacity crowds; it is hard to picture a talk explaining historic Protestantism's role in shaping society and culture drawing much of an audience. The "other" had come to be most near; the "marginal" was, if not central, then at least to be reckoned with along with heirs of the old "center."

Where does the new situation leave America today?

First, most Protestants have widely accepted the pluralist situation. One could ask: What choice did they have? In the nineteenth century Margaret Fuller, on visiting Britain, once pronounced, after due consideration, "I accept the universe." Ralph Waldo Emerson is remembered as having said, "Gad, she'd better." Diversities among peoples, interests, and religious groupings is part of the mental furnished apartment in which citizens live. It is not going to disappear. People might wish it away, define it away, keep their distance from the fellow citizens they find too different, seek to control immigration, close their eyes to reality, but such efforts will be to no effect: The "other" is here to stay.

Still, the acceptance has been more hearty and less grudging than we might have expected when compared with how peoples have interacted in other places and at other times. Internationally, interreligious hostility has at least partly inspired or legitimated most war during the past fifty years. Nationally, the United States, with its history of Protestant crusades against Catholicism, various anti-Semitic outbursts, religious justification for slavery and segregation, and elimination of Native Americans or the confinement of them to reservations, should have expected more hostility.

Despite such an expectation, opinion polls show that at least mild tolerance prevails. Certainly, anti-Semitism has not disappeared, and anti-Islamicism is present in the current climate of crisis. Yet discrimination not only has *not* been a part of state policy but also has been militated against on legal grounds. As noted in the previous chapter, almost no dead bodies have accrued due to interreligious strife during the last half century in the United States, certainly not as many as can be counted in any day's newspaper when compared with the number around the globe.

In fact, accepting the "other" religiously has become one of the *creencias*, with its corresponding *vigencias*, of the culture. No one is surprised to read of Hindu-Muslim conflict on the Asian subcontinent, Jewish-Muslim conflict in the Middle East, Protestant-Catholic conflict in Northern Ireland, or everyone-against-everyone conflict in the former Yugoslavia. Moments of peace and gestures of peacemaking in such places are what make news. In the United States the rare moments and actions of interreligious hostility are the news.

The American scene in which Protestants had such a major shaping role is in some way viscous, plastic, and flexible. To some this openness results from a waning of commitment among the Protestant majorities. Their cynical critics like to suggest that *real* religion *should* inspire persecution and harassment or at least unwelcoming of the "other." If you *really* believed, says the taunter, you would develop the absolutist and lethal elements of your scriptures and tradition and try to rule out the "other." However, though many hard-line Protestants may sound belligerent, publish tracts critical of differing beliefs, and work out proselytization strategies in the name of their own exclusivism, not much more happens than the passing of those tracts to people of other faiths or the occasional doorbell ringing. None of their actions are the stuff of history; such actions do not make headlines or even footnotes.

To paint with such a broad brush is to risk being accused of Pollyannaism, of glossing over abrasions, because one can always adduce inconvenience, sometimes adduce pain, and on rare occasions adduce true violations of civil codes and the manners of civility. Yet before one writes with a fine-tipped pen, the broad brush can provide a useful background.

Is this climate of acceptance of the "other" something about which Protestants should boast? Is this openness innate in the Protestant tradition? Hardly. Lutherans and Calvinists and Anglicans and Presbyterians engaged in open conflict; they killed often the heretic (think Servetus) or the rival sect (think Anabaptists). One has to use acute eyes to find exceptions, people favoring tolerance, mutual hospitality, interreligious discourse, and the lowering of barriers in the longer Protestant past. I have read the evidence dug up by searchers for such persons. Reinhold Niebuhr found a few in the left wing of Puritanism—John Saltmarsh was one name that got preserved in my notes for Ph.D. examinations.

Here and there, Quakers enlarged the concept of religious hospitality and then made room for others, as they did in Pennsylvania. Now and then, Baptists, in the name of "soul liberty" and freedom of conscience, were open to pluralism, as they were in Rhode Island. Certainly, when colleagues in the Protestant Enlightenment came along, Quakers and Baptists linked with them to promote religious liberty and create a climate potentially friendly to realized pluralism. New England Baptists Isaac Backus and John Leland at the side of Thomas

Jefferson are examples. Most New England Congregationalists and southern colonial Anglicans were slow to make the
moves that eventually came to characterize America.

Still, these Protestant seeds were contributors, as were the
products of Enlightenment founders. The U.S. Constitution,
with its Article 6 ruling out religious qualifications for hold-
ing office and its First Amendment committing the Congress—not yet the states—to religious freedom, played its
part. The practical situation played a role among a practical
people. To form a union was practical, and that could not happen if religious monopolies endured. To avoid bloodshed was
practical, given the example of the Thirty Years' War on the
European continent and the constant bloodletting as England
worked toward toleration after 1688. To allow for and even
welcome uncongenial immigrants, such as Catholics, was
practical, as such peoples made up the labor force in the cities.

We might say that America "lucked out"—some might say
this was God's blessing, or Providence—with its constitutional
provisions and its constant influx of new peoples of diverse
faiths. That luck continues in the new century. Though black/
white tensions and hostilities make up the great tragic flaw of
American life, for the most part non-Protestants and non-
white Protestants find or make their home in the mix. Citizens
who are alert to the *vigencias* may bristle at legislation dealing
with affirmative action or Title 9, promoting gendered parity
in public college athletics. Yet resisting engagement is "just
not done around here."

Actors and actresses, musicians and athletes, and other pop culture celebrities can be quite open about their born again status, their commitment to Judaism, their heritage in an Asian religion. Transplanted forms of Zen Buddhism and Hindu meditation become campus and living-room fads. Younger generations may have trouble even finding credible hostilities such as the massive Protestant anti-Catholic expressions from before Vatican II. Space does not permit a full-scale examination of whether something about Protestantism allows for these attitudes of change. Mainline Protestantism certainly finds such attitudes easier, yet often conservative Protestants, for whom decades ago the pope was the veritable antichrist, now form coalitions with those they once called papists to promote causes, such as antiabortion. And the same Protestants, for a variety of theological and political reasons, may be friendlier to Jews on Zionist causes than many liberal internationalist-minded Protestants might be.

My remarks so far have made life in pluralism sound easy, but there are obvious countertendencies. Two of these, the "politics of resentment" and the "politics of nostalgia," mentioned earlier, are present in new-millennium Evangelicalism especially. Whining, griping, moaning, whimpering, and complaining about the loss of life in the Good Old (Protestant?) Days, as of the 1950s, such voices claim that America until then represented a coherent, graspable past. People agreed with each other. They were all devout, until the secular-humanist- and pluralist-favoring Supreme Court in 1962 and

1963 took God out of the schools. The citizens had prayed in school.

Did they? Studies of America just before 1962 found that only 2 or 3 percent of the California school districts and only 10 or 11 percent of the Midwest districts had school prayer. Opponents of the decision only noticed that they missed school prayer when they could not have it, by court decree. Support for school prayer amendments comes from those areas, often in the American South, where relative homogeneity survives or where particular forms of Protestantism remain dominant in the statistical makeup and ethos of a region. The chief justice of the Alabama Supreme Court defied the U.S. Supreme Court by mounting his hand-carved Ten Commandments (in Protestant translation) on his courthouse walls. When challenged with the charge that such an action is offensive to non-Protestants, non-Christians, non-Judeo-Christians, he asserted that this was a Christian nation, not a Hindu or Buddhist one. Such an assertion can be wildly popular where the politics of nostalgia rule. The judge could not safely speak in such terms in San Francisco; Los Angeles; Washington; New York; Dearborn, Michigan; or thousands of other, often smaller, communities.

If once people were "all devout" because they were homogeneously Protestant, advocates of this tradition also say they were "all moral." Such advocates are not silly: They do not claim that there was no crime, that prisons were empty or not needed. Rather, they say that certain "absolutes" promoted by

Protestantism contributed to the *consensus juris* that made legislation promoting morality popular. In pluralist America, making the case for this or that particular moral-minded legislation is more difficult. The charge of nostalgists is that pluralism promotes relativism.

The diversity and contention present in Protestantism in the era when the citizenry was apparently devout, moral, and homogeneous gets overlooked. Again, when were more Americans agreed on who God is, what Jesus Christ does, why the Bible is true and capable of settling arguments, and whence morality flows than in Protestant America 1861–65? Yet both sides legitimated their policies, proslavery or proemancipation, secessionist or unionist, to the point that rivers of blood flowed and oceans of ink were spilled. Protestantism may have been a big tent, but it had many smaller tents under its canopy.

Admittedly, good arguments are more difficult when the parties involved cannot agree on which texts to fight over. Father John Courtney Murray once said that Americans think they are arguing when they are simply in confusion. Having some sort of text over which to argue is precisely what is lacking in a culture where "secular" (read, by its organized enemies, as "secular humanist") texts mix with texts that are Jewish, Christian, Muslim, Hindu, Buddhist, New Age, and so on. Murray said that to have an argument people must ascend into some sort of metaphysic or ethic or theology, which is precisely what pluralist societies cannot provide.

Alasdair MacIntyre, after surveying the pluralist scene,

called his book *After Virtue*. The title is a pun, of sorts. He meant that citizens are going after virtue, seeking it, searching for standards. But he was also referring to chronology: Citizens are too late to find virtue. Philosophies on which people might once have agreed, be they Aristotelian, Thomist, Natural Law, or we might add, biblical, in all its varieties, no longer serve across boundaries. Too many people, too many religions, have rejected what these coherent philosophies offer or are unmindful of them and could not grasp or accept them even if they were mindful of them.

It is on this scene that the pro–Ten Commandments forces have moved from the politics of nostalgia or resentment to the politics of will-to-power. (I know that to mention politics is to deal with will-to-power; what else is politics?) But this will-to-power comes from people who previously disdained the notion that they were part of such movements. Now they have gone public and turned political in organized, overt ways. It is in this context that support for school prayer amendments, for the Ten Commandments on a courthouse wall, for a crèche of Jesus on a courthouse lawn, for legislation favorable to the "Judeo-Christian tradition," all find their place.

To move so quickly past Murray and MacIntyre is not to say that they do not have valuable points. They have placed urgent items on the national agenda, an agenda I cannot pursue in detail in this treatment. Even the more militant groups that wish to return the nation to an idealized past and that would privilege, where they cannot establish, the Protestant (codified as the Judeo-Christian biblical) tradition serve enlivening purposes. The issues they raise are often valid and are by no means addressed with the attention they deserve. The task in this book, however, is to set up signs and pointers, and one of the big ones belongs here: Can particular Protestant resources, whether these come from liberal, mainline, Evangelical, Fundamentalist, African American, or other roots, contribute to what are now often the battles of bumper-sticker emblazoners and interest groups?

Protestants of all sorts will not be able to be on the sidelines for this reason: They have all gone public. Even the Amish, who will not represent themselves in court, make legal history, as others stand in and stand up for them. Zoning battles, issues of tax exemption, and debates over religious rights and religious freedom are all very much a part of Protestantism gone public. When the Protestants ran the show more significantly, many of their efforts could pass as private. Indeed, in my own earlier works over forty years ago I spoke of most Evangelicals as devoted to the private. They wanted to keep an "enclave culture," to be unspotted by the world. In these earlier works I quoted evangelist Dwight L. Moody, who said that the world was in a flood (of sin), and God had given him a lifeboat with a command, "Moody, save all you can." Such Protestantism, often with an eschatological and even apocalyptic bent, looked for the imminent return of Jesus and saw itself as an urgent rescue mission. Why try to promote social gospels, to improve the world, or to work for world peace, when the church had a different mission?

Protestants not in the Evangelical camp also often defined themselves as private enclaves in their congregations and denominations. Churches would indeed equip their saints to go out of the sanctuaries and be good citizens, but in the division of labor, they left to political, economic, social, and academic agencies the task of dealing with politics, economics, social concerns, and academic interests. Religion was for weekends, families, private life, and residential existence. It was not for the crossroads. Certainly in the age of conservatives in local churches, elites in denominational task forces or bureaucracies and activists in publishing houses, academies, or interest groups might have advocated movement into the streets, markets, or classrooms, but they were not central to the church's mission and, in times of social unrest, were often kept at a distance from ordinary congregational life.

Now, even though mainline Protestants are much less visible than they were on the social-action front in the days of the civil rights movement or when their denominations had more means and more power, in their congregations most of them have taken on public missions. They often play a larger role than Evangelicals in dealing with the "other," in promoting interfaith activities, and in interpreting life positively within a pluralist society. A role reversal has taken place as the once-private party has now produced for the public arena a Moral

Majority, a Christian Coalition, overt support of the Republican Party, market awareness, entertainment (Christian rock), celebrities, scandals, rallies, slogans, and music (soul, gospel, spiritual, often borrowed from African Americans).

I seem to be lapsing—I *am* lapsing—into or reverting to the conception of two-party Protestantism, when, in actuality, as I have noted, there are many parties, not only among Protestants, who range from conservative Evangelicals to more liberal Methodist thinkers, from African American activists to Amish and Mennonite isolationists, but also among the citizenry, who range from Catholics and Jews to Muslims, New Agers, and Buddhists to atheists and agnostics, which begs the question: Is there even a tent?

Several years ago I teamed up on lectures with an international economist who addressed audiences with a good news/bad news duality. The good news was that the market had won. The Soviet Union had imploded; China had turned capitalist, albeit without freedom; radical socialisms were on the defensive. My colleague was from the University of Chicago, where if one says that often enough he or she may win a Nobel Prize.

The bad news, he went on to say, was that Americans have not the faintest idea with what personal, social, cultural, and religious philosophies—he used the plural—they are to greet this triumph. He was aware that a single philosophy—be it communist, Maoist, fascist, nazi (shall I add capitalist?)—was unfreeing. Yet some sort of coherence, he implied, had to exist if America was to serve creatively on the international scene.

Since he spoke, the dot.com crash, the Enron/Arthur Andersen/Merrill Lynch and many others scandal, and the like, have led many to lose faith in the market that has won. The 9/11 terrorist act, inspired by religious fanatics, led many to see that religion as such may not be part of the solution and certainly could be a part of a desperate problem. In reference to the emerging global scene, the more than 100 million Protestants are dispersed among the philosophies and indifference that go into life in a republic. Many of them, on many levels, will find company with non-Protestant, nonreligious people and groups. Others are interreligious in new ways. They are challenged by individualist spiritual seekers who reject Protestant signals. Will Protestants find their place?

On the American scene, Protestants are busy regathering, trying to rebuild community in a time of individualist emphases. Without community, the Protestant spirit and what is valuable in its heritage cannot sustain itself. Though mistrust of religion in the face of militancy and scandal has grown, an opening for Protestants to be heard exists. Though the culture is likely to be moved mainly by "secular rational" thought, many aspects of life are not covered by such thought. On life and death issues, people reason also on the basis of community, scripture, tradition, memory, affection, and hope. Protestantism is on a landscape where the debate over whether a tent is or should be over the show they used to run is often preoccupying.

My own approach is modest: Rather than have imperial

ambitions, to be moved by nostalgia or resentment, it seems best in the mean time to draw on motifs of Protestantism, elements of community, scripture, tradition, memory, affection, and hope, that can see to the survival and invigoration of the Protestant subcommunities in their tattered tents, where the flaps flap in every breeze. From there I can move to meet other kinds of Protestants, other people of other faiths, under a sky that offers little protection, but where sun and light often break through in a dark time.

Creencias and *vigencias* tend to have an open, moving (if slow moving) character. They are dynamic, subject to change and growth. If the bad news is that our culture has little idea with what outlooks to greet the new time, Protestants would ill serve their heritages if they abandoned efforts to address situations in public life, while tending—as they often have more elegantly—the spiritual and existential questions evoked within private and personal life.

They can address the basic public issues: saving the environment; sustaining development; addressing the growing gap between the overfed and the ill-fed, the rich and the poor; assuring rights; finding better ways than warfare for resolving conflicts. Their God—don't all Protestants believe this?— is the Lord of history, the God not held captive in the sanctuaries, but who in mysterious ways leads his people to address the world that unfolds before them, a world their ancestors helped shape, a world their ancestors managed, controlled, and directed, as their children cannot so readily do. And if my historical accounting has some merit, it is a world in which Protestants should not aspire to run the show but to serve where they managed, to partner where they controlled, to co-operate where they directed.

If Pastor Robinson was right, that "the Lord hath more truth and light yet to break forth from his holy word," there should be some fresh things to say, to do, and to hear.

INDEX

African American religion, 12, 20,
23, 42, 44, 50, 57, 60
After Virtue (MacIntyre), 73, 74
Alabama Supreme Court, 72
America Comes of Age (Siegfried),
14
American Way of Life, the, 53
Amish, 11
Anabaptists, 11, 69
Anderson, Arthur, 78
Anglicanism, 4, 10, 47
Anomie (de Grazia), 39
anti-Catholicism, 3
anti-Semitism, 67
Apologia of Robert Keayne, 46
Aristotelian philosophy, 74
Asian immigrants, 55
Autobiography of Malcolm X, 31

Backus, Isaac, 69
Baptists: in colonial America, 10–
11, 46–47; influence of, on belief
in freedom, 28, 69; and origin of
Fundamentalism, 6–7; as
Protestant faction, 20
Beecher, Henry Ward, 39
Beecher, Lyman, 39
Berger, Peter, 9
Bible, 13, 16–18, 30
black Muslims, 57
Block, James, 33
Bonhoeffer, Dietrich, 32
Boorstin, Daniel J., 24
Boston, 46

Boundaries (Lifton), 61
Brauer, Jerald C., 30
Brotherhood Week, 50, 55
Buddhism, 72
Bush, George W., 61
Bushman, Richard, 45

Calvinism, 22, 26, 49
Carson, Rachel, 5
Catholicism: and anti-Catholicism,
3, 42–43, 47–48, 67; beliefs of,
18–19, 25, 27, 28; denominations
in, 13; government of church in,
16, 24; and immigration, 4, 42–
43, 70; mainstreaming of, 26, 49–
50, 53, 63, 66
charismatic groups, 11. *See also*
Pentecostalism
Christian Century magazine, 56
Christian Coalition, 59, 77
Christocentrism, 26
Church of the Brethren, 11
Coffin, William Sloane, 60
Congregationalism, 10, 70
consensus juris, 64
Constitution, United States, 36,
42, 69
"constrictive" approach, 62
Consultation on Church Union
(COCU), 56
Council of Trent, 18
Cox, Harvey, 60
creencias, 22–35, 50, 54, 65, 68, 79
Culture Wars, 63

Index

Das Kapital (Marx), 5
de Grazia, Sebastian, 39
Disciples of Christ, 11
Divine Principle, 31
Dutch Reformed Church, 11
Dutch West Indies, 45

Emerson, Ralph Waldo, 43, 67
Encyclopedia of Religion, The, 8
England, 41, 42
Enlightenment, the, 13, 37, 38, 42, 47, 63, 69
Enron, 73
Episcopal Church, 4, 10, 47
Evangelicalism, 15, 20–21, 27, 29, 54; and politics, 55, 59, 61, 71
Exclusion Act, 43

Feminine Mystique, The (Friedan), 5
Ferdinand, King (of Spain), 41
First Amendment, 36, 47, 69
France, 41
Franklin, Benjamin, 42
Friedan, Betty, 5
Friedman, Milton, 5
Fuller, Margaret, 67
Fuller Seminary 20, 21
Fundamentalism, 6, 7, 20, 44, 48

Galbraith, John Kenneth, 5
Germany, 11
GI Bill, 44
Gilded Age, 43
Goldwater, Barry, 59
grace, 18, 19
Grace Cathedral, San Francisco, 32
Graham, Billy, 9, 56, 58, 66
Great Society, 55
Greek Orthodox, 13

Hawthorne, Nathaniel, 43
Hebrew Scriptures, 42
Herberg, Will, 5, 38, 44, 52, 53
hermeneutics, 17, 18

Hinduism, 68, 71, 72
Hispanic Pentecostals, 21
Hitler, Adolf, 5
Hobbes, Thomas, 33
Hollinger, David, 58
Holmer, Paul, 32
Holocaust, 54
Holy Roman Empire, 41
House Un-American Activities Committee, 24
Huguenots, French, 42
Hunt, Robert, 4

"infidels," 47
Iowa, 11
Isabella, Queen (of Spain), 41
Islam, 12, 41, 66, 77
Israel, 54; God's covenant with, 31
Ivy League schools, 50

Jamestown, 4
Jefferson, Thomas 42, 69
Jewish-Muslim conflict, 68
Jewish people. *See* Judaism
John XIII, Pope, 20
Jones, (Dean) Alan, 32
Judaism, 13, 25–29, 43, 53–54, 63, 71, 77; and anti-Semitism, 67
Judeo-Christian tradition, 44, 53

Keayne, Robert, 46
Kennedy, James, 61
Kennedy, John F., 55
Keynes, John Maynard, 5
King, Martin Luther, Jr., 27, 60
King James Bible, 7
Küng, Hans, 60

Leland, John, 42, 69
Lifton, Robert Jay, 61
Lincoln, Abraham, 25
Luce, Clare Booth, 56
Luther, Martin, 27
Lutheranism, 11, 19, 23, 32, 57

DATE DUE